ASTRAL PROJECTION

Development for Mystical Spirit Walking & Out of Body Experience, Day & Night Meditation, Hypnosis & Affirmations

(Master Theta, Delta & Lambda Waves, Journey Beyond Your Physical Body)

Gertude Shofner

Published by Tomas Edwards

Astral Projection: Development for Mystical Spirit Walking & Out of Body Experience, Day & Night Meditation, Hypnosis & Affirmations (Master Theta, Delta & Lambda Waves, Journey Beyond Your Physical Body)

ISBN 978-1-989744-85-7

Legal & Disclaimer

The information contained in this book is not designed to replace or take the place of any form of medicine or professional medical advice. The information in this book has been provided for educational and entertainment purposes only.

The information contained in this book has been compiled from sources deemed reliable, and it is accurate to the best of the Author's knowledge; however, the Author cannot guarantee its accuracy and validity and cannot be held liable for any errors or omissions. Changes are periodically made to this book. You must consult your doctor or get professional medical advice before using any of the suggested remedies, techniques, or information in this book.

Upon using the information contained in this book, you agree to hold harmless the Author from and against any damages, costs, and expenses, including any legal fees potentially resulting from the application of any of the information provided by this guide. This disclaimer applies to any damages or injury caused by the use and application, whether directly or indirectly, of any advice or information presented, whether for breach of contract, tort, negligence, personal injury, criminal intent, or under any other cause of action.

You agree to accept all risks of using the information presented inside this book. You need to consult a professional medical practitioner in order to ensure you are both able and healthy enough to participate in this program.

Table of Contents

Introduction

This book contains proven steps and strategies on how to induce an astral experience. I personally guarantee that as you give your full attention to this book you will achieve an astral experience before reaching the end.

I have dedicated the last 40 years of my life to exploring transcendental experiences which most people will never have the courage to even attempt.

I congratulate you on taking a journey which will amaze and surprise you beyond anything you can imagine.

Thanks again for downloading this book, I hope you enjoy it!

Chapter 1: What Is Astral Projection?

You've obviously picked up this book because you are interested in astral projection. Astral project can prove to you that you are more than just a physical body, more than just the muscle, tissues, sinew, bone, and fat, and something more. Astral projection can also show you many different other realms that you can explore in the astral plane, such as the dream plane, or any other place in our universe. The world of astral traveling is complex and intricate, but hopefully with this book you may find it to be a bit easier to understand, and develop ability to travel there. Why would you want to travel there?

You may find out more about yourself or others by exploring these planes, and uncover secret knowledge that may be thought to be hidden from the seeker. Knowing you are not just a physical entity can reveal to you the real potential of an afterlife, or life past this physical vessel. There are even occurrences of people using astral projection to witness their past lives. You may also meet spirit guides who live in different planes that may guide you on your quest as to what you may seek. Astral projection may also give you a sense of tranquility that has eluded you throughout other areas of your life, also bringing clarity to the question of who are we, what are we, and what is our purpose. However, before you can dive into figuring out how to perform astral projection, you need to know exactly what astral projection is so that you can find out if this is for you or not.

So before we begin, what are some reasons to not learn astral projection? The most obvious being while you are out of your physical body, it could be harmed on the physical plane. If you die on the physical realm and your astral body is not in your physical body, yes, you will die in real life. This is a danger that anyone takes when in a deep meditation or trance. There is also the potential of having your "astral cord" cut, severing your connection to your body. That is also a possibility. You need to guide yourself and protect your cord when traveling in the astral plane by calling upon angels, the archangel Michael, Jesus, Buddha, or other ascended beings to help protect you. There is also the possibility of meeting dangerous demonic entities while traveling in the astral plane that may want to server your cord or do you harm, even consume your life force. Again, if you protect yourself and call on holy entities to protect you, your astral body, and physical body, will be unscathed. But we'll talk more about that later. With all these warnings aside, let's learn more about astral projection.

Astral projection is known as an out of body experience. In other words, it is a separation of your astral body from your physical body. Once the two have separated, your astral body will then travel to an astral plane. In this realm, you can communicate with spirit guides and deceased loved ones, travel to the several heavenly realms, and even spy on a cheating mate. However, the latter is not recommended. You want to respect everyone's privacy.

Astral projection is something that a lot of religions tie to the afterlife because your astral body is traveling to another realm. Very often astral projection is reported to be associated with your dreams or a form of meditation that you have done or are doing. That is potentially why there is the possibility of learning more about yourself and others in the astral plane, much like in a dream, or higher state.

Some people have reported similar perceptions of astral projection being induced by hypnotic (self-hypnotic) or hallucinogenic means. However, scientific evidence cannot back this up or prove that there is any way for your soul to separate from your body. Any scientific evidence of astral projection is known as pseudoscientific. But there are reported incidences of real astral projection defying science and describing locations accurately, or providing accurate details about one's surroundings. There are many cases when medical patients on the verge of death have experienced an OBE, or out of body experience, and accurately described the work of their doctors while under anesthetics or comatose.

Chapter 2: Initial Steps In Performing Astral Projection

The answers to the questions posted on the previous chapter remains debatable up to the present day. This is because the number of experts who believe that astral projection can be taught and learned is almost in equal measure with the number of people who believe that astral projection can only be successful if it is a spontaneous experience that is without any prior learning for the person who is undergoing the out-of-body experience. Regardless of whatever has been proven by scientific research and what astral projection experts believe to be real, the number of instructors who specialize in teaching the art of astral projection to those who are truly interested to learn.

The first step for projecting the astral self is to prepare oneself for the process while in a relaxed state. It is best to do this mental preparation during the early morning hours when the individual has just awakened and is still drowsy with the remnants of his sleep. Dawn is also believed to be the best time for the individual's awareness to be in its most relaxed state. As a matter of fact, this is backed scientific studies that state the human brain is in its most active state during the hours of 3 to 5 or 6 in the morning. Despite this high level of activity, the brain is also at its most sponge-like quality, able to absorb all the information that is fed onto it.

Waking up in the morning also has another benefit for the preparation process, and it is that the individual is located in a part of his home where his defenses are down most of the time. In order for the individual to be able to successfully project his astral self, a state of deep relaxation is required. This is best achieved when the individual is in a room where the atmosphere is less stress-inducing. Married couples who are still learning the basics of astral projection also have to try doing it solo first. This is because it is easier for human consciousness to slip into a relaxed state when there is no one else in the room as compared to when there is an observer or two. This may mean that during the first few months of the astral projection apprenticeship, couples may have to sleep in separate bedrooms.

Another important factor that would aid the individual in achieving the highest level of relaxation while trying to do the astral projection is to minimize the distractions as much as possible. This means that he has to lower the shades on the window to block out the sun’s rays and remove any object from the room that may cause a distracting noise. It is also important for the astral projection rites to be done in a room where people are less likely to barge into, a fact that couples who have kids would surely understand.

Without any disrespect intended for children, it is a fact that they can be the biggest distractions to a parent who is trying to relax. So people who wish to practice astral projection may have to think twice before embarking on this path, especially if they have infants who are in need of constant attention.

Chapter 3: How To Get Started?

We have talked loads about what is astral projection? The beliefs about it, the five bodies, and also the benefits offered by it. But now the main issue is - How to astral project actually? What next is to how to reap those advantages!

Well, as easy the concept is, that very easier are its methods to go about it.

The first basic and the most important requirement is to be a good sleeper. One should be able to have a sound and a deep sleep to be able to project well. To enhance your sleep, suggestions of a few aids are given so that you can have a great time in your dream world!

The choice of the aids should also be very well made on the basis of your sleep. The choice of a 'DEEP' sleeper should differ from that of a 'LIGHT' sleeper. Yet, the mind of the both should be awake.

The right kind of balance has to be maintained between the sleep and the mind. The quality of projection totally depends upon the person's ability to keep his body at rest and himself asleep, yet, the mind awake. This mode can be attained easily with the help of the projection aids mentioned above. A deep sleeper would feel comfortable with the mask whereas a light sleeper might go in for some other option. Also, it is not good to sleep very deeply because our ability to enter into astral life slackens.

Let us discuss in detail how to get started on astral projections.

How to Get Started?

Now, the next topic of our concern is the **steps involved in astral projection**. The aids give us an idea about how to project effectively, whereas the steps required in this procedure would further brush up our practice. Many people have not been really successful in carrying this out which is mainly due to not following the essential steps. Adhering to the steps will help people to experience a phenomenal out of the body experience.

Anyone wanting to experience an astral projection must follow the following steps:

Relaxation and Proper Breathing

Spiritual Cleansing

Protection through White Light

Raising our Kundalini

Energizing our Astral Body through the Kundalini

Preparing the mind for Astral Travel with Self Hypnosis

Lastly, Astral Projecting!

Step 1: Relaxation and Proper Breathing

Firstly, one must be totally relaxed and should practice proper breathing. Relaxation is a very important ingredient of this experience. It is the most common area of people's failure. One's mind needs to be at rest and the whole concentration should be on the projection and not on other petty issues.

All the ladies especially, if you are very keen to get through this experience, forget about those incomplete house chores, the broken plates and the crying child! Just focus on this task first and then the rest of the tasks.

The correction of breath on other hand is also a must to obtain a proper way and an approach to effective projection. Practice of different types of breathing is highly recommended to become calm and be in a position to astral project. Proper breathing would help you to release the mental and the physical pressure off your bones and experience the new you, the new world.

Step2: Spiritual Cleansing

First of all, what we mean by spiritual cleansing is that removing all the deadlocks and the negative emotions sprouting up in our mind so that we undergo an inner transformation and are able to understand ourselves better. Once we are spiritually cleansed, we begin to receive both conspicuous and inconspicuous benefits. The benefits which are visible are conspicuous and those which are invisible are inconspicuous. Most importantly, apart from these benefits, the most important benefit is an internal cleansing is done which removes all the hindrances of development and projection as well. People might be able to astrally project but they might not experience the best results. The main reason is that they are not spiritually awakened.

They say that 'birds of same feather flock together' or 'like attracts like' i.e. people with same attitude would form a group; the one's with same likes or dislikes form another group. Similarly, negative emotions attract negative vibes, whereas, the positive thoughts attract positive vibrations. It depends solely upon us what we prefer to choose. If we have a lot of negative vibrations within us, we would vibrate the same in our environment. Hence, to have a best and positive experience, we have to mould ourselves like that.

Step3: Protecting Ourselves Using White Light

White color is symbolic of purity and serenity. If we remain in touch with the white light, half of our problems are resolved!

White light gives us a lot of positive energy and also offers protection from the negative bodies or energy surrounding us. It also serves the purpose of an energy booster by supplementing our energy. There is a level appraisal to the point where the negative emotions and energies don't exist. So, we are able to experience a better projection due to the high state of life.

Step 4: Raising and Energizing our Kundalini

This is the key to a successful travel. Kundalini is an extremely powerful source and force which is full of unlimited energy which has to be energized time and again for a good experience. The ways to energize the kundalini are many; some common ones among them include yoga or meditations which cleanse our chakras.

This step also involves a similar performance as done in the previous steps above. The raising up of the kundalini raises the energy levels to such an extent that it becomes very easy for the astral body to escape into space and make a travel. High energy levels are related to high levels of vibration which act as an incentive for the astral body to easily escape the physical self. This prepares our mind and body for a new experience hence, the step has to be properly performed with wisdom.

Step5: Preparing the Mind for Astral Projection with Self Hypnosis

The next step towards a good travel is preparation of the mind for astral projection with self-hypnosis. It is the best way to get rid of the fears that hinder a person's growth. The person is also encouraged to build a positive outlook and maintain high energy levels that not only keep him charged up throughout but also help him to have an incredible experience.

Step 6: Astral Projection Finally!

Last but not the least you are ready to experience a travel. Travel to the world you want to, meet the people you want to. Acquire attributes and talents that you have always wanted to.

Chapter 4: How To Train Yourself For Astral Projection

Training To get into the realm of Astral, there are some major training requirements that you must meet. 1. Make sure that you are in 100% relaxed state when you are awake. 2. Make sure that whatever you are doing has all of your attention. 3. Have some physical energy in your body 4. Try to make your astral body project out of your physical body. These four steps when performed together will help you in triggering an Astral Projection or an Out Of Body Experience (OOBE). The exercises that can help you in calming down, concentrating and entering the state of projection are discussed below. 1. Relaxation Full body relaxation exercises are important and they prove to be quite useful. If there is one you already know, you can make use of it. Otherwise, here is one that can be used to relax your body:

Sit down or lie down and focus on your feet. Now, completely make them tense and then release the tension by relaxing them. Once you are done with feet, move on to your calves and then thighs and so on. Target each set of muscles one by one and repeat the process until you feel completely relaxed. Remember that a deep state of physical relaxation is essential for achieving a state of trance and reaching the astral dimension gets much easier from the state of trance. 2. Contemplation Clearing your mind of random thoughts is essential and one of the basic purposes of meditation. As soon as you try to meditate, many different thoughts will start to surface. They will crowd you and make you pay attention to them. However, what you need is to get rid of them and pay full attention to projecting your astral body out of your physical one. To get rid of these thoughts, the best idea is to understand them and resolve them. Think about the one that bugs you the most. Think about it for a long time and think about it deeply to gain insight about it. Once you have dealt with your thoughts, you can move on to the exercises that help you in clearing your mind so that you can direct your attention on projection. 3. Breath-Awareness Meditation This form of mediation lets you clear your mind. Here is how you practice it. First relax your body using the relaxation exercise mentioned earlier. Now, take a deep breath and feel it going in your lungs. Pay full attention to breath entering and exiting your lungs and don't think about anything else. Repeat this process for a long time and you will be able to push other thoughts that may distract you out of your mind. Using this exercise, you can think on a deeper level because your surface mind is now occupied by it. 4. Surface Thoughts Sounds are among the most distracting mediums as they can lead to surface thoughts. For instance, the voice of a person can generate thoughts like "Who is this person?" and "What is he saying?" etc. You have to learn to ignore these sounds and use them to strengthen your concentration. Instead of using different sorts of music to cover these sounds listen to these and ignore them. This way, you will be able to master different sounds and resist them from interfering in your concentration. 5. Concentration Concentration is the basic idea of all this training. You need to totally concentrate and focus all your powers on what you are doing. For a successful projection what you require is all of your concentration and mental power. All steps that you follow in the process of projecting in the astral require your concentration. Here is a simple test for checking your concentration. Sit down in an easy state and relax. Now, close your eyes and do not think about anything. Start breathing deeply and count your breaths. Keep counting your breaths and make sure that there is nothing else on your mind. As soon as a thought drifts you from counting your breaths even for a second, start counting again from the beginning. Being able to go for at least ten breaths is a good practice but it is not enough. However, even if you are not able to get to ten, you can improve yourself with these exercises: Concentration Exercise – 1: In a calm environment, place a light source, preferably a candle and stare at it for some time, like a minute or two. This will leave an image in your mind once you close your eyes. Now focus on this image as hard as you can. Try to keep this image in your mind and keep viewing it for as long as it is possible for you. Instead of letting it fade away, try to use your mental powers to make it grow without opening your eyes. You can call this exercise "After-Image Retention". Concentration Exercise – 2: A person can better his concentration with this exercise in which he is required to continuously stare at a spot on the wall.

You have to just keep looking at the spot and not concentrate on it. Your mind must be blank, and gazing is all you should be doing. Just keep looking at it and whenever a thought crosses your mind, just get rid of it without letting go of the spot. Keep doing this for as long as you can patiently do it. Since this exercise is pretty easy, you can do it multiple times each day. Concentration Exercise – 3: Sit down and relax. Don't think about anything and close your eyes. Focus on your breaths and imagine that the air that you inhale is full of life energy and it is of your favorite color. Breathe it in and imagine getting energized due to it. When you breathe out, imagine that the exhaled air is colored gray and it is full of the waste matter and negative energies of your body. This exercise purifies you and allows your chakras to get energized. Remember that in the beginning, these exercises might be a burden for you as you are required to stop thinking about anything but as you keep doing these exercises, you will realize that in fact, it is easier to clear your mind and not think about stuff. As you continue, you will find it quite relaxing to clear your mind. Trance State When you truly relax your body and calm your mind down, you will start feeling heavier than usual and it will keep getting heavier. This heaviness tells you that you are starting to enter the state of trance. You feel heavy because your brain waves are changing due to a deep form of relaxation. This is quite normal and you shouldn't worry about it. What it means is that your mind is fully conscious, but you are sleeping. How to Enter a Trance With your breath awareness and relaxation exercise, calm yourself down. Now think that there is the ladder that you don't see and you don't have to see. Imagine it in total darkness and start climbing it down. Synchronize your movement with your exhales i.e. with each exhale, climb down a few steps. What you need to achieve is the effect of you falling down. If you are doing it right, your brain will change its state from awake to asleep or even deep sleep. When you feel that you are in the trance state i.e. you start feeling heavy, you can stop imagining about the ladder climbing. Other than a ladder, you can think about a life or you can think of yourself as a feather. The purpose is to induce a falling effect in your mind so that it helps you in going into the state of trance. When you are in the trance, you will feel a difference in everything. It all gets quieter and you get the feeling of being in a very big place. Your body feels like vibrating slowly and one can feel things getting blurry. Deep Trance There are different levels of trance and the one you achieve depends on how relaxed, committed and experienced you are. The beta level is the one in which you are awake and alpha is the one in which you are asleep but theta is the level of deep sleep and to achieve this level, you have to keep exercising for a longer period of time. As far as projection is concerned, you can do quite well even in the state of normal alpha level trance and there is no particular need for deep trance. There are some symptoms associated with deep trance and you can observe them tell if you are entering that state: • You feel cold but without any sort of shivering due to it. • You feel like losing the heat from your body. • It feels that everything is happening at a slower rate than usual. • You feel unattached from your body. • Unable to move your body i.e. a feeling of paralysis. You can feel some of these symptoms even when you are in alpha state but when you are entering the deep trance state, the symptoms will be much stronger and you won't be able to mistake them. You will at once know that you are entering the trance state of deep sleep. Furthermore, you will be needed to work for it and it is not like you just get into it without putting any effort. Another important thing is that you don't have to worry about it because any time you feel uncomfortable you can get yourself out of this feeling. When you feel uneasy, try to move one of your toes or fingers and when you are able to do that, focus your energies on moving your body parts and you will come out of your sleep. Energy Body Expansion When a person first enters the trance state, he starts losing control of the body and starts vibrating all over. After that, it appears as if the body is expanding. All these symptoms indicate that you are in your normal process of sleep. In this state, your energy body actually expands to accommodate more energy so that you can project into higher levels. This is called energy body expansion. Trance Familiarity It is easy to get out of the state of trance unwillingly because most people are not familiar with it and they think that they have actually initiated their entry into the astral realm. Since this is not true, they end up making themselves unstable in the trance and hence they wake up or get out of it. If a person is able to maintain his posture and stay stable both mentally and physically in the state of trance, he can keep it going for longer periods of time. First-timers enter this state and as soon as they realize that they are in this state, they get over excited and try to get to astral as soon as they can. This increased excitement becomes the reason for ruining a perfect opportunity. Those who enter this state for the first time will do good to remember that calmness and stability are the keys. Try to maintain your concentration and get familiar with the state so that you understand the feeling of it. Always remember the following tips: • Trance just helps you learn the way of energy and chakra. It is not a necessity. • Best place for trying to get into this state is on a comfortable armchair. When you are in a trance, you will realize the astral projection of your body is quite loose and so to gain movement control in the astral dimension, you will need to project your arms and legs out of your body by slowly lifting them. For this, you don't have to move your body muscles because that can lead you to break out of the trance. All you need to do is to concentrate and focus on feeling your arms and legs in the astral body. Tactile Imaging A person is able to perceive the presence of his body and different parts of it. For example, using your hands, you are able to tell the different parts of your body and their approximate distance from your hands and this is known as Tactile Imaging. When you are supposed to be aware of yourself and the parts of your astral body, you should pretend that you will touch the parts of your body using your imaginary hands. You don't have to move or try to move your actual arm and hand muscles. With your eyelids close, try to hold out your hands and imagine their position. Move your arms, twist your wrists and turn your hands and in the meantime, keep concentrating on their position. In the same way, you can go over different parts of your body and feel the sensation with the concentrating power of your mind. This practice allows your mind to fully concentrate on the area that you feel like touching and that way, you will be able to move your imaginary hard just with the power of your mind. Following the same practice, you can move awareness from one part of your body to the others and use it to help you in your projections practice. Remember that while you are doing this, you don't even have to keep an image of your body parts in your mind. You just have to pretend that you are feeling them moving around and touching other parts of your body. Blind people, especially the ones who are born blind, don't have the powers of visualization, but they do have a sense of awareness. They are aware of their parts of the body just like a person with sight when his eyes are closed. The problem is that most of the projection techniques make use of visualization and this makes it difficult for blind people to work on these techniques. So, the technique of tactile imaging that is mentioned is very handy for people who are blind as well as for those who have sight.

Chapter 5: The Supplement Approach To Lucid Dreaming

"Lucid dreaming has considerable potential for promoting personal growth and self-development, enhancing self-confidence, improving mental and physical health, facilitating creative problem solving and helping you to progress on the path to self-mastery."
-Stephen LaBerge, PhD

Until recently, people had to go to great lengths in order to have lucid dreams. It used to be that only with consistent practice every day could you expect to have such an experience…. not to mention that such dreams would often be difficult to control and hard to remember in the morning.

The great news is that there are much smarter ways to go about your lucid dreaming practice. I'm going teach you everything you need to know in order to start lucid dreaming through the power of natural herbs, but first, I want you to know how this approach came into fruition.

This approach:

After learning about lucid dreaming, like many of you, I was completely fascinated by the idea. I was in high school at the time and my cousin had recently started experimenting with lucid dreaming and astral projection. As he told me about these incredible dreams he was having I couldn't help but feel this deep intrigue emerge within me about the idea. It sounded surreal at first, but I soon began experimenting with various techniques and was utterly shocked to experience my first lucid dream within just a couple of weeks.

Over time I came to realize just how amazing these dreaming experiences can be. I quickly learned that anyone can learn how to lucid dream. And that is something I actually want to reiterate to everyone reading this book. ANYONE CAN LEARN HOW TO LUCID DREAM.

While I did find certain lucid dreaming techniques to be quite helpful at inducing lucid dreams such as dream journaling, meditation, and reality checks in particular - I sought to go deeper. I read everything I could find on the subject - articles, books, forums, blogs, etc.

One day, I came across a scholarly piece that discussed the role of natural supplements for lucid dream induction. The idea of lucid dreaming supplements sounded interesting so I began experimenting on myself. I started looking deeply into dietary supplements and their effects on the dreaming brain and was surprised to find that I was not alone in my attempt to understand the properties of supplementation for lucid dreaming. Quite a few academics had actually explored the subject extensively. I soon came to understand exactly what needed to happen in order to become lucid in a dream and how various supplements could be used to achieve such success.

Over time I started helping others experience lucid dreams through the use of these natural herbs I had learned so much about. I developed a clear understanding of how to subjectively approach each supplement depending on what the dreaming experience was like for from the night before for all kinds of different body types. Progressively I began helping people have more and more amazing lucid dreaming success.

But using herbs to enhance the dreaming experience is actually nothing new. People all across the globe have actually resorted to natural herbs (some of which I will cover here) for centuries to help them have dreams at night, even lucid dreams. (And just to clarify, I'm not talking about questionable herbs either; I'm talking about herbs you can literally find at your local health food store.)

These herbs have helped me and thousands of other experience lucid dreams on a regular basis and they can help you too. The supplement approach to lucid dreaming described here will show you how to combine several of these amazing herbs to optimize successful and high level lucid dreams. This approach has consistently provided shocking results not only for myself but for just about everyone I know who has tried it.

Chapter 6: How To Develop Psychic Abilities

Psychic ability is what is commonly referred to as intuition. Intuition may be described as the ability to discern future events. It is a different kind of sense. It is the sixth sense which science seems to acknowledge that it exists but has no way of proving it. Intuition suppresses logic. It also exceeds an educated guess.

Source of Intuitions

Although it is not easy to define intuitions within particular frames, there are some conventions that can be witnessed about the occurrence and manifestation of intuitive acts. People who are considered to act intuitively, or even do some actions that are perceived to be out of the ordinary, perform the acts within the following parameters that often directly relate to their current manifestation of psychic power.

*Past experiences
*Present moments
*Subconscious instincts; these are also commonly referred to as gut feelings.
*Intuitions and the Self

You must also come to the realization that some emotional responses are not really ours since forces outside of our system trigger them. Often, we are conditioned by society and friends to adopt certain responses to stimuli around us. Yet, deep within us, we know that the response does not sit at the center of our being. In other words, we are not comfortable. You must learn to develop your own responses as opposed to the conditioned one that only inhibits your power to access your inner powers such as psychic ability.

Types of Psychic Abilities

Clairvoyance

Clairvoyance is derived from two French words coined to make one meaning. The words that form it are clair (French for clear) and voir (French for see).

It is the ability to see events that will happen. It is a psychic power that is made use of by leaders around the world to help them forestall future activities. It has been argued that clairvoyance can only be used positively.

Clairaudience

This is the ability to perceive sounds from the outside world. It is similar to clairvoyance but it is about perceiving the sounds with your auditory senses. People with clairaudience may experience these sounds quietly in their mind but often report hearing them practically in their ears. It is a gift of the psychic and can be accessed through the process described for psychic activation.

It must however be mentioned that whereas each of us has the ability to practice and exercise these psychic powers, they still tend to run in some families. It is yet to be established whether it happens inherently or whether it is through encouragement and nurturing of such powers. The greater weight however falls on the side of inherent abilities, with an admission that nurturing also plays a role in the manifestation of these magical powers.

Clairsentience

This is the ability to feel the emotional states of others in the past, future or present. People who manifest this psychic power can retrieve information from houses, private buildings and even guarded premises with sheer mind retrieval force.

Psychometrics

The term is coined from two Greek words that mean the mind and measure. People with psychometric abilities are able to discern what others experience from a distance. Such people make use of items used by the subjects to make intuitions about them. Such items could be a chain they have previously worn, a cloth or shoe. It can even be a letter written by the subject.

Extra Sensory Perception

This psychic ability is also known as cryptesthesia. People who manifest this psychic power are able to acquire information without the use of any of the five conventional senses. Apparently, we are all born with this ability. Children are said to possess this power and exercise it without inhibition but they soon lose it after the age of 4 years. They lose it because adults are constantly trying to condition their minds. However, some children continue with the power until adulthood. It has been observed that some families nurture the gift. In other cases, the psychic power appears to run in families with such families commonly referred to as ESP families.

Telepathy

Telepathy is a form of extra sensory perception. It has to do with direct communication between two living beings on a level that is void of any verbal discourse or written contact. It has been demonstrated that telepathy may occur between humans and humans or humans and animals. Recent evidence shows that indeed telepathy is an advanced sense commonly used by animals among themselves.

Precognition

In this type of psychic ability, you can perceive future events through extra sensory perception. Such people usually develop what is commonly referred to as a hunch. They perceive the occurrence of an event beforehand.

Now that you have seen the different forms of psychic powers that you could nurture, how can you start nurturing these powers to your benefit? Gemstones have the hidden treasure in unleashing the inner psychic power within you. Let's now learn about how to unleash your immense psychic power through gemstones.

Chapter 7: What You See

Synopsis

If we speak of a man as rising from one plane or sub plane to a different, we don't think of him as necessarily moving in space at all, but instead as transferring his consciousness from one level to another—bit by bit becoming unresponsive to the vibrations of one order of matter, and beginning instead to answer to those of a higher and more refined order; so that one world with its scenery and inhabitants would appear to fade slowly out of his view, while a different world of a more elevated character would get through .

The View

We must mention first that every material object, every particle even, has its astral twin; and this counterpart is itself not a simple body, but is commonly exceedingly complex, being composed of assorted kinds of astral matter.

Also each living creature is surrounded with an atmosphere of its own, commonly called its aura, and in the case of humans this aura forms of itself a really fascinating branch of study. It's seen as an oval mass of luminous mist of extremely complex structure, and from its shape has occasionally been called the auric egg.

The universal life-fluid as it is absorbed and specialized, as it circulates in rosy light throughout the body, as it eventually radiates from the healthy individual in its altered form, is also perfectly obvious.

Most bright and most easily seen of all, maybe, though belonging to a more polished order of matter—the astral—is that aura which expresses by its bright and ever-changing flashes of color the different wants which sweep across the man's mind from moment to moment. This is the true astral body. But to see these, the student must, naturally, have developed the vision to do so.

One additional point deserves mention in connection with the appearance of physical matter if viewed from the astral plane, and that's that the higher vision when amply developed possesses the power of magnifying at will the minutest physical particle to any wanted size, as if by a microscope, though its magnifying power is hugely greater than that of any microscope ever made or ever likely to be made.

It will by this time be obvious that although the average objects of the physical world form the background to life on particular levels of the astral plane, yet so much more is seen of their true appearance and features that the general effect differs widely from that with which we're familiar. For the interest of illustration take a rock as an illustration of the simpler class of objects.

If regarded with trained sight it's no mere inert mass of stone. Firstly, the whole of the physical matter of the rock is seen rather than a really, small part of it; second, the vibrations of its physical particles are detectable; third, it's seen to possess an astral twin composed of assorted grades of astral matter, whose particles are likewise in constant motion; fourth, the universal life is seen to be circling through it and radiating from it; fifth, an aura will be seen encircling it, though this is naturally much less extended and altered than in the case of the higher realms; sixth, it's appropriate elemental essence is seen penetrating it, ever active but ever vacillating. In the case of the vegetable, animal, and human realms, the complications are naturally much more numerous.

An account of the scenery of the astral

plane would be incomplete without a little mention of what have frequently, though erroneously, been called the Records of the Astral Light.

These records (which are really a sort of materialization of the Divine memory—a living photographic representation of all that has ever occurred) are truly and permanently impressed upon a very much higher level, and are only reflected in a more or less spastic manner on the astral plane, so that one whose power of vision doesn't rise above this will be likely to get only occasional and disconnected pictures of the past rather than a coherent narrative.

However nevertheless these reflected pictures of all sorts of past events are constantly being reproduced in the astral world, and form a crucial part of the surroundings.

Chapter 8: Astral Projection Basics

Everyone is capable of astral projection but not everyone does experience it. For one, you need to be willing to cross over from the realm of the living where you exist in your physical body, to the realm of spiritual existence. As a beginner, there are three steps that will help you manage this transition. Those three steps include taking off; managing to stay in your lucid state; and being able to remember your experience on the astral plane even when you have resumed your physical state.

How to take off

This is the very initial stage and it is all about relaxation. You need to be fully at ease; not tension in your body. You also need to be relaxed at a mental level. It is difficult to succeed in making an astral journey when you have endless thoughts disturbing your peace. Only when you are fully relaxed will your astral body – the one that also goes by the term psychosoma – be ready to take off. And your relaxed astral body needs to be accompanied by a relaxed energy body – what also goes by the reference energosoma.

When it comes to energy flow, do whatever you can to have your energies well distributed. One great way of achieving this is to address the issue of your chakras – those energy fields, which when blocked deter the smooth flow of energy. The reason your energy arena is important is that your energy body is the link between your physical body and your astral body. So, whereas opening chakras is not often mentioned as a pre-requisite for astral projection, having your chakras open and your energy well balanced helps your attempt at astral projection. You realize you aren't exactly free as your chest is being suppressed by a feeling of heaviness; as if something with a big weight has been placed on it.

Remaining lucid after take off

What would you say lucidity is? Well, it is the state of being awake and conscious, even when you have abandoned your physical existence. Saying that you need to be lucid after take-off means that you need to be conscious of what is happening around you in the new sphere that you have entered. Do not confuse that with registering what is going on around your physical body. Lucidity is important for you to be able to see things in the astral sphere and even to be able to interact with other astral bodies. Your lucidity is what will make you have something to bring back in form of memories about your astral travel.

Remembering your astral experience

Whatever you see and hear when in your astral body is not registered in your physical brain. Rather, it is recorded by your parabrain, the extra-physical brain that operates in your psychosoma or astral body. Hence, for you to be able to personally analyze your out-of-body experience, or even narrate it to anyone, you need to have those memories transferred from your parabrain to your physical brain. This memory part is important as not all astral travels are for leisure. There are times you can have an experience of astral projection and come back with useful information from some astral bodies or even from some friendly spirits.

Luckily, there is a way you can rehearse for your astral travel in advance, so that whatever you experience is not just well recorded but also nicely transferred to your physical brain at the end of your astral journey.

Create a phrase or sentence that has useful meaning.

Keep the phrase or sentence simple

A good example of such a sentence is: I will be lucid when I conclude my astral journey and I will recall everything on return to my physical body.

Say it aloud to yourself.

Say it with energy.

Repeat it a number of times, say, five to ten times.

After you have set your body and mind into a state of relaxation, repeat the phrase to yourself again, still aloud.

During your out-of-body experience, make a deliberate effort to note the names of people and places that you see and keep affirming to yourself that you are going to remember them later.

What happens on returning to your normal state is that the information regarding your astral experience is transferred from your extra-physical brain to your physical brain; and it helps if you manage to make a deliberate transition yourself from the astral realm to the physical world. In short, having your brain jogged back to reality of the physical world by a siren or an alarm can sabotage your memory. So you need to try and deliberately bring yourself back to your physical existence, all the while keeping your focus on the recall process.

Helpful Tips As You Prepare For an Astral Experience

Reading material such as this which is contained in this book is a good move because when it is time for you to embark on your astral journey nothing will really shock or scare you. It is also good to slow down and think about your life as it is as well as the experiences you have gone through. That awareness may help you to make sense of some things that you see in the astral world later on. It is important that you appreciate that each person's astral experience is unique. As such, you need not try and replicate someone else' experiences or experiences that you have read in books. Those other experiences can only help you to prepare for the journey psychologically.

Be open to a personal experience

In that regard, do not try and manipulate experiences in the course of your astral journey. You should be calm and relaxed and ready to sail with the tide during your astral travel as long as you are not encountering anything evil. What you see while in the astral world could be very enlightening for you when you return to your physical world still lucid and with vivid memories of that astral experience. You have to have your own astral experience to understand what an astral journey or astral projection really is.

It is as simple as when it comes to eating – can you really tell what it's like to eat meat if you've been vegetarian all through your life? Only if you ultimately eat meat will you be able to tell how meat tastes like. And you can then take someone through the digestive experience and even explain how different it is from when you have consumed vegetables alone. Again, only your personal astral experience can help you make conclusions about your life.

Identify a suitable technique

Just because you know someone who succeeded in astral projection using a certain method is not enough for you to go with that particular method. With the choices provided in this book, you should be able to find your own fit. Among the things you need to take into account is your personality. Consider, for example, how creative you are; how rational you are; and even what your preferences are. You may wish to use a technique that has breathing moves or even meditation while someone else may not like it. So consider the techniques at your disposal and then test the waters and see which technique you can handle without feeling anxious.

Once you have identified the technique that suits you best, practice it beginning from the first part; its middle part; and its final part. As you will notice as you continue learning the different techniques of astral projection, each one of them takes you through a process. None of them is like a switch where you say let me transition to the astral and you got there – no. So, do master all the stages until you can do them without being too conscious that you are doing them. As a beginner, it is best you keep off those techniques that seem complex and somewhat mystical; they can be discouraging.

Another important thing you need to do is to go through a period of practice – one month is recommended. During this period, you choose some days in the week when you can practice going for an astral travel using your chosen technique. Whatever day you select, do the astral projection just once. Spread the days of practice as you like, but ensure you have practiced fifteen times in that one month. By the end of that month going for astral travels will no longer feel strange or scary to you.

Bear positive emotions

Being positive of your impeding journey helps you have a great experience. It also helps in your take off stage so that you do not have to struggle to get started. So as much as possible, let yourself be filled with quality thoughts and balanced emotions. Such emotions include confidence; perseverance; self-motivation; persistence; curiosity; and such. The contrasting emotions that you need to avoid include self doubt; fear; anger; distracting thoughts such as busy thoughts unrelated to your astral journey. Depending on the activities lined up for the day, identify an appropriate time for your astral projection – a time when you feel you can easily relax and guide your thought process accordingly.

Choose a suitable environment

First of all you need to relax as has already been mentioned before. For that matter, it is important that you choose an appropriate environment for your astral experience. A place with a door, for instance, is great because you can always lock everyone else out to avoid being distracted by in and out movements when you are in the middle of your session. The temperature also needs to be suitable – neither too hot nor too cold – all in a bid to keep you comfortable. 20°C is deemed suitable.

And you need to be able to regulate lighting. The ideal place for an experience in astral projection is one that is dimly lit. This means you can switch off the electric lights and then light a spotlight or light some candles and place them in strategic locations in the room. Do whatever else you need to do to avoid distracting noises. For example, if you have an alarm clock or a mobile phone, they are best switched off or put in silent mode if possible. It may be difficult for you to remember properly what transpired in the astral arena if you are jolted into the real world by an alarm. Generally, a quiet and comfortable place is recommended if you want to succeed in relaxing and remaining calm all through your experience; and if you want to have your memories from the astral world intact when you resume your physical existence.

Note the recommended time

When you are practicing astral projection, it is good to set aside enough time for it so that you do not feel constrained to go through a technique in a rush. At the same time, it is not good to overstretch the period for an astral experience. So, although you are bound to get the hang of it in due course, as a beginner you need to do some timing. Keep your session to a minimum of half an hour and a maximum of one hour.

Although some people speak of setting an alarm, you need to be alive to the fact that you do not want to be sharply jogged back into the real world. So you may wish to try timing yourself with something like a mobile phone where you can choose some form of music for your alarm. Such an alarm is likely to be friendly to the ear and likely not to negatively affect the transfer of your memories from the extra-physical brain to the physical one. Once you have set your alarm to ring after one hour, relax and proceed to do all the steps that your chosen technique avails. Then transition back to the real world carrying back the images and sounds from the astral arena.

Sensations that are not physical

As you study different techniques for astral projection, you may be warned about what to expect. However, it is good that you know what to generally expect from the time you begin preparing yourself to the time you resume your natural physical existence.

Expect to feel sensations that are not physical; some being vibrations, others kind of electric sensations, pressure within your forehead or even at the back of your head, and so on. Do not panic as these sensations are normal before and during the transition period. In fact, they are just warnings; indicators that you are on the right track to astral projection. The sensations actually manifest as your astral body tries to disengage from your physical one. Whatever you feel, it is good to note it down when you return from your astral travels, together with the things that you saw and the interactions that you made. While recording astral experiences is not mandatory, it is good to have such a record to compare with future experiences. From them, you also get to understand your pattern or patterns of transitioning from your physical world to your spiritual world.

Chapter 9: Practice Makes Projections

Now that the foundation is laid out, it doesn't seem so otherworldly. It's tangible. I encourage you to interact with others on the subject. Find social media groups (I found a great Facebook group that expedited my initial research). This book alone is intended to guide you into this path. It is not all inclusive, as I have much to learn myself. Teaching is one of the best ways to learn, so here I am today!

Meditation:

Meditation is key for many to achieve the Hypnagogic state. This I struggled much with at first. No matter what I researched I kept finding tutorials, guides, and instructional information that all lead to: "clear your mind".

WHAT DOES THAT EVEN MEAN? Well after much frustration and repeatedly "not getting it", I had a revelation. I had realized for me personally, as I am constantly thinking and have racing thoughts, that "clearing my mind" simply meant letting my thoughts run free. I didn't have to turn them off to clear my mind like the word *clear* implies.

Now when I meditate I let my thoughts run rampant while distancing my consciousness from them. Basically, let them go. This detachment is not only key for meditation, but also for mastering your own emotions as well. Just like that guy in a galaxy far-far away once said. "Attachment leads to jealousy, the shadow of greed, that is. Train yourself to let go of everything you fear to lose."

In a not so sci-fi kind of way, mastering this "Zen" is ultimately what allows control of one's consciousness, and ultimately sub-consciousness, which is exactly which we must tap into in order to trick our body into sleep while our mind remains awake. The seven Chakras are also something you will want to understand and practice. Chakra(ˈCHäkrə): each of the centers of spiritual power in the human body, usually considered to be seven in number. Chakra is an old Sanskrit word that literally translates to wheel.

This is because the life force, or prana, that moves inside of you is spinning and rotating. This spinning energy has 7 centers in your body, starting at the base of your spine and moving all the way up to the top of your head.

Remember: "The higher power in which we all seek is simply the existence of all the collective energy in the universe."?

Often, many will have a more dominant chakra, as I doubt we can be in perfect balance without practice. For me it is the sixth Chakra.

Ajna : The Third Eye which translates to "beyond wisdom."

This chakra opens your mind to information beyond the material world and the 5 senses.

Extra sensory perception, intuition or psychic energy, all comes from the third eye.

There is a small pinecone shaped gland in your brain that takes in light. This gland, the pineal gland, is responsible for helping you feel awake in the daytime and sleepy at night.

Long before brain imaging, ancient cultures knew this Third Eye existed, and they also realized that it receives information from sources outside of the five senses.

I must add, that even as I write this and sharpen my research, I make new connections and have new understandings of my own experiences.

That being said, I have found through meditation, I can channel energy to my 3rd eye deliberately and quickly just by focusing on that physical spot and imagining a clockwise rotation

This is something tangible that I can feel, sometimes overwhelmingly. However, up until now, I was not aware that Chakra translated to wheel, and that prana moves and spins. That just goes to show how such a process can be so exciting.

Life is all about connecting the dots. When we gain new knowledge, we use what we have already learned to do so. Again, like the way we put words to thoughts See all of these connections?

Chapter 10: Starting Out

Once a person goes to sleep, the astral body is projected into the physical dimension. It is able to freely move around, but a limitation is caused by a field of energy of the expanded body. This field is called the cord activity range. When a person is trying to project into the astral dimension in his consciousness, there is a phase in which the person is on the horizon between the astral and physical dimension. Beginners often black out and miss this phase. Etheric Matter All the living creatures contribute to the generation of a matter existence that is responsible for life force and this matter is regarded as the Etheric matter. It is both physical and astral in nature. In the past years, scientific studies have proved the existence of this matter as it carries weight. People who die lose a bit of their weight precisely before the moment of death and the reason for this is that the

Etheric matter from their body is transferred from physical to astral body. This also happens in the near death experiences. Manifestation of Dimensions All non-physical entities require some Etheric matter in order to function properly closer to the physical dimension. If there is no Etheric matter associated with them, these entities fade back to the dimension from where they originated in the first place. This matter is redundantly available in the physical world and it can only be obtained from here. Flow of Energy The flow of energy between the physical and astral body is carried out using the Silver Cord. Just like an umbilical cord, it not only ties the two instances of a body but also regulates the energy flow between the bodies. The projector is often able to view the cord and where it connects the bodies. This also depends on the beliefs of the projector and his chakra system. A body in astral dimension needs energy from the physical body to sustain it in that dimension properly. If there are no proper reserves of energy, astral body will get weaker in the astral dimension and the person will not be able to remember things from that dimension just like in the real world where if a person hasn't eaten in days, he tends to get weak and sleepy and face problems in interacting with it. What it means is that the flow of energy must be properly coordinated so that the astral body is able to give you vivid memories of the stuff you observe in there and it stays in your physical mind when you get back to the physical world later. Use of Chakras Being able to fully control and use the chakras is a long process and take years of practice to perfect. But it does not mean that you need to fully master it before having your Out of Body Experience. There are some basics that can help you reach the first few stages with a good energy flow. You can change and take control of your lucid dreams and your astral experiences by learning the control of your energy flow through the chakra points. Using this, you will be able to experience another life in a whole other dimension and you can use that to grow and learn in both dimensions. Higher Levels Just like the astral level, there are other levels as well in which a person can exist. These have various different names that are jotted down here for you in order: Adi, Anupadaka, Atmic, Buddhic, Mental, Astral, and Physical. To reach these levels, a lot more consciousness is required. Each of these levels have some areas that lie between the two adjacent levels. These are also known as buffer zones. To understand it properly, think of Earth's atmosphere as the Astral dimension and if you wish to go into Stratosphere which can be considered the buffer zone in this example, you will need to have a body designed for it i.e. a jet plane and to go to the Mental level or outer space, you will need a spaceship or a Mental Body. Entering higher levels and their buffer zones requires a certain amount of energy and there are techniques that can help a person move from physical dimension to the next levels. Projection into the Higher Levels To produce energy for entering the higher levels, a fine control over the chakras is required. With fine tuned control over these chakras, an individual is able to produce the energy that allows him to reach the next level and be conscious in it. There are a number of techniques for the awakening of awareness and mastering these techniques can lead to controlled projection and experience of the higher levels. The astral body is the basic one and the rest of the bodies such as mental are a part of it. If the individual has a right amount of energy, he can project astral body in the astral dimension and this astral body projects other bodies in their respective dimensions. When this happens, a person is able to experience multiple realms and dimensions at the same time and that gives him memories of all these dimensions in just one projection. However, the memories that are most dominant are the ones that are experienced by the body with the highest amount of energy. Projecting into higher levels requires a lot of skill and experience. The person must be able to control his chakras and his consciousness. Although it takes time, it is not impossible. People have been practicing this for years and they have experienced these levels and wrote about them. Projecting into Atmic, Buddhic, and Mental and Astral level is something that a lot of people experience. However, the next two are not among the most visited ones. Astral Dimension In this dimension, you can observe things as they are and they appear to be very real. However, as soon as you wish them to change, they change. You can experience whatever you want to experience in this realm. Time is extended and is perceived at a lower rate than in the physical world.

You can imagine beautiful sceneries and they will appear right in front of your eyes. You can give yourself super powers and enjoy them. In the astral dimension, there are dream pools but for most beginners it is not easy to journey as they plan. For having such a journey in there, you need to be very experienced at this. When you are having a dream, you are just viewing it without being able to control it. If you mind is strong enough to take control of your awareness from your subconscious during that time, you can view whatever you want to view in your dream. How to Project into Virtual Reality This is a very easy method of creating a personal realm for an individual. What you need is a poster of natural scenery, one that is quite sunny and bright. Make sure that it is at least the size of a standard poster but if you can get a bigger one, that would be better. You will need to put it on the wall of the room in which you plan to project and position a spotlight such that it illuminates the poster when all other lights are off. Now, what you need to do is to make sure that there is no other light in the room and then turn on the spotlight. Now, slowly walk towards the poster without thinking about anything and just keep going. As you slowly go towards it, your subconscious will perceive it as a realm instead of a 2D poster. Just keep trying and soon you will find yourself in the poster's realm and you won't be able to tell if it is real or a creation of your mind. This is an easy and effective method and also allows you to customize your realm by choosing a scene with more people or objects in it. Moreover, you can cut objects from other pictures and paste them on your poster and they will become a part of your realm when you step into it.

Chapter 11: Lucid Dreaming Techniques

1. Dream awareness method

This method is relatively simple and require self-observation and keeping track of your dreams. I would suggest some sort of dream journal, if you will. Whenever you remember a dream, just write down details such as location, characters, feelings and other things that you consider important to your dream.

Next thing, you should focus on, is reality checks. For example, I always looked at my feet and I asked myself:" Is this a dream?". Sometimes, I would count to ten. I'm sure this doesn't make a lot of sense, but look at it this way, in dreams time and any kind of image of yourself will be pretty blurry, therefore you will be able to tell the difference. You can also pinch yourself if you want to, from my perspective it doesn't really matter as long as you do it 3-5 times per day. Whole point of this, is to create a routine. Once you do your daily routine unintentionally, same will apply to dreams and hopefully you will be able to realize that you are in the dream, and take control of the situation.

Some people try to recognize their dream "signs", such as running away from monsters or falling into darkness. I couldn't find any signs that were common in my dreams so I just skipped this step, but if you have such "signs" that are common I'm sure they will help greatly. Don't think about it too much, do your daily routine and try to write down common things in your dreams. Not everyone finds this method useful, I would suggest experimenting to find what method suits you best.

2. Wake back to bed method

Lucid dreams, and vivid dreams in general, almost always occur during REM sleep, the deep sleep phase characterized by Rapid

Eye Movement. The first REM phase typically occurs ninety minutes after you first fall asleep, with additional phases roughly every ninety minutes afterward. The goal of this method is to wake up during a REM phase, then fall back asleep and continue the dream aware that you are dreaming.

There are many ways to increase the amount of REM sleep you get. One of the most effective, and the one that causes REM sleep to appear at regular times, is to stick to a daily sleep schedule, and to sleep long enough that you wake up well-rested. Set one alarm to go off either 4.5, 6, or 7 hours after the time you fall asleep. You're more likely to be in REM sleep during these times, although it's difficult to predict in advance. The six or seven hour times are the most likely to work, because later REM phases last longer, and are more likely to contain vivid or lucid dreams.

Write down your dream if you were having one, make yourself a snack, or just get up and walk around for a while. Your goal is to get your conscious mind active and alert, while your body is still full of sleep hormones. Close your eyes and fall asleep again. If you remember the dream you were having, recall it and fall back asleep, imagining yourself continuing the dream. Even if this takes quite a while to happen, you've got a decent chance at a lucid dream.

3. Additional methods

Meditate.

Before going to sleep, meditate in a quiet, dark room. Taking a meditation training course may give better results, but to start out, just pay attention to your breathing, or imagine ascending or descending stairs. The goal is to stop thinking and enter a quiet, comfortable state, and from there slip into a lucid dream.

Prolong a lucid dream as it starts to fade.

One common experience among first-time lucid dreamers is waking up due to the excitement of having a lucid dream!

Usually, you'll get some warning before hand as the dream feels "unstable" or you begin to notice sensations from the real world. These techniques can help you keep the lucid dream going

Listen to binaural beats.

If you send a different sound frequency to each ear, your brain will interpret the two sound waves overlapping pattern as an audio beat even though no beat is included in the sound. This definitely changes the brain's electrical activity, but so far scientists are unsure whether this can actually stimulate lucid dreaming. There are many websites out there with collections of binaural beats, so it's easy to try it out if you can sleep with ear buds in. Most would-be lucid dreamers use beats that mimic Theta brain waves, which occur in REM sleep, but some swear by Gamma or Alpha beats instead, or a progression through several types.

Chapter 12: Experiencing A Higher Consciousness

Ask as many alternate consciousness experts out there for an advice on astral projection and you will get all sort of answers. Some of these responses are new. Some were discussed here, but there is one thing about achieving success in astral travel they all agree with: EXPERIENCE HIGHER CONSCIOUSNESS FIRST.

A higher consciousness is key to an effective astral projection. It frees you within and not from anything. It makes you lighter as you let go of any excess baggage you carried on from the real world. As you become lighter from within, your energy flows more fluidly to help you travel to the metaphysical universe.

There is no step-by-step process in experiencing a higher consciousness. You are only required to have a positive perspective. Below are some tips to help you shift your view of the world and yourself to their more positive side.

Live in the moment.

There is no use living in the past, especially if it is something unpleasant or regretful. Remember what you learned from the experience, but let go of the negative memory.

What is important is your now and how you can control it to determine your future.

Remember that there is only you in every moment.

Not to be mistaken as self-centeredness, this only means you need not compare your life journey with the people around you. Comparison only leads to misjudging or doubting yourself.

Denounce your fear of self-discovery.

The human mind is like a large castle with many rooms. Some of these rooms are lit, others are not. The rooms that are dark represent the part of your consciousness you are still afraid to visit.

When you begin your journey to experiencing a higher consciousness, you need to visit the dark rooms in your mind to allow some light to get in. This will enlighten you with other things you never knew you are interested in or capable of.

When you visit the dark rooms of your mind, even some of the long-forgotten feelings are renewed. Have you been so focused at work, you forgot to feel the joy of just seeing the sunrise or hearing the hush of the wind through the trees? Maybe this feeling is locked up in one of the dark rooms of your mind and just needs to get out of that door and in to the more accessible parts of your mind.

Be identified as nothing.

At this day and age, everyone and everything is identified with labels. When you are trying to experience a higher consciousness, you must be a human being and not just someone with this

specific name, gender preference, job, race, or religion. These labels will only limit you from discovering more about yourself.
Remember that no one is perfect.
You are completely human and not being the best in anything does not make you any less.
Strive to be perfect but do not expect perfection. You will only be disappointed.
If you are disappointed, it is easy for negative thoughts to invade the consciousness. Then if these thoughts start to clutter your consciousness, it will be difficult to rediscover yourself and your entire being.
Create change by understanding your reaction instead of focusing on the person or thing that made you react.
When something happens to anyone, especially if it is unpleasant, their instant reaction is blame the person or thing that triggered it.
In raising your level of consciousness, you need to analyze why you reacted the way

you did. This is instead of trying to point fingers at someone or something. Knowing the reason behind your reaction helps you revisit issues that are still hounding you up to this day and finally give them closure.

Just like astral projection, experiencing a higher consciousness could not be achieved overnight. You will stumble upon challenges along the way, especially in breaking bad habits and facing the fear of self-discovery. With patience and faith in yourself though, realizing a higher consciousness would not be for long.

Chapter 13: Returning To Your Body

As wonderful as an astral experience can be, there always comes a time when you must return to the physical world and care for yourself and loved ones. As sad as it may be to return to the world of the mundane, know that you will always be able to return later.

Knowing When to Come Back

Time does not exist in the astral realm, so it follows that it is very easy to lose track of it when you're out exploring the cosmos. While this isn't usually a big deal if you don't have any obligations for the rest of your day after your travels, your body might object to being neglected for hours at a time. Remember the importance of nourishing and hydrating your physical body to stay in the best shape possible.

As pleasant as it may be to free yourself from the weight of the physical world and explore the universe unbound, spending too much time in the astral realm is generally not advised unless your occupation is spiritual in nature. Spending an excessive amount of time out of your body will not only take its toll on your physical form, but it can also loosen your grip on physical reality. You can have a hard time focusing on your job and your obligations to yourself and loved ones if you're constantly dreaming about going back to the astral realm.

We are all spiritual beings having a human experience in the physical realm, it is true, but we also had very specific reasons for coming here, and they all involve actually experiencing the physical. For this reason, you must remember to spend the majority of your time here, where you originally intended when you decided to come here.

To prevent staying longer than you want or is safe for your body, set a timer with a loud alarm to alert you when your journey must come to an end. When first starting out, you'll want to set the timer for a shorter amount of time and work your way up to a longer time, never exceeding two hours before you come back for a break. If you decide to return again after your two hours are up, be sure to drink some water, eat a snack, and go to the restroom before you go out again.

The Return Journey

The return from astral travel can be very easy and straightforward. Simply think about your physical body and you will immediately go there. Some people snap back into it spontaneously as soon as they see their bodies, but others will need to lie down in themselves to get back in.

Others need a more progressive transition to return, as the suddenness of snapping back in can be jarring and unsettling. Shamanic practitioners especially use a method to transition back before returning to their bodies. For a longer return process, you can simply retrace your steps and go back the way you came. You can set your timer to give you a single warning beep so you know it is time to start transitioning back, with the final alarm going off when it is time to be in your body and return to awareness.

Grounding

Once you return, it is crucial to ground yourself in your body. Move your fingers, arms, feet, and legs to get accustomed to being physical again. If you experience sleep paralysis when you first return, shake your head and limbs until you regain control over your body.

Sit up when you come back to alertness and do a grounding meditation. You can do this meditation sitting or standing. Envision roots sprouting from the bottoms of your feet and stretching down into the earth. Plunge them down all the way into the center, then begin drawing energy up from the Earth's core into your roots. Starting at your feet, slowly fill yourself with this earth energy, all the way up until you reach your head. Take a few deep breaths and slowly return the energy down, until you feel solid and grounded. Repeat as many times as necessary.

After Care

Be sure to eat and drink as soon as you return to your body. Nuts and fruits can help connect you with earth energy to further ground yourself. If you're having a very hard time getting grounded and shaking off that floaty, woozy, feeling, eat some meat to help lower your vibration back to normal.

If you find yourself coming back exhausted from your travels, let yourself sleep as much as you need. Don't deny your body the opportunity to balance out again and recharge. It takes a lot to get used to this level of psychic work, so be gentle with yourself, take good care, and stay healthy.

Chapter 14: Apt Preparation For Astral Projection

Some things are easier said than done; you agree, don't you? Like someone telling you, never mind, you'll get another one, after you have lost your gold necklace to a street urchin. **Never mind**...seriously? Yet, difficult and even illogical as it may be, there is a technique you could learn that helps you to let go of even those things that look humongous to your spirit.

Here are some things you have learnt are necessary for your success in astral projection, yet they are not necessarily the easiest to achieve; things you will learn how to accomplish in a moment:

Having your body in its entirety in a state of complete relaxation

Attaining full level of concentration in whatever move you make

Being full of energy to be able to tap from a rich source as you balance on your silver cord

Being able to instigate pressure on your astral body so that it leaves your physical body when you want it to.

As mentioned earlier on, these are beautiful states that make things right in astral travel, yet you will only achieve them when you know how. And the how-to includes activating your chakras or energy points so that there is abundant energy flowing to create a path and give momentum to the astral body. How to get into the requisite state of trance is a skillful art you need to learn.

Here is how to enter the right state of mind and do things right:

Relaxing

Choose early mornings for your sessions of astral travel. That is the time your muscles are relaxed and your mind is so drowsy it has not begun to awaken to the thoughts of the day's awaiting challenges. You also are not tired and so it is easy for you to concentrate on whatever you direct your mind to. Such early times of dayare the best for you to manipulate your inner self with least resistance or distraction.

To curb fears

Have you ever tried to trace a place and after weaving your way through streets and alleys you finally located it? How excited you must have felt! But then come your return journey, and GPSs were nowhere around... Making your way back can be even more frustrating than the initial headache of locating the place. Incidentally, the same thing can happen in your attempt at astral projection – your spiritual body makes it out and finds it difficult to return! When else do you think panic sets in if not times like these?

In order to remain relaxed in the middle of your astral travel, it is imperative that you do not panic or develop anxieties. One thing you can do is to ensure that you venture just within your area. In short, avoid daring yourself when you are new to this astral experience. Trying to fly to another state, whomever you think you could find, should not be your priority right now. It is enough that you walk around your room trying to locate your reading lamp, your favorite shirt or dress, and so on. Gradually you will be able to move to your other rooms and back into your physical state with confidence. And in due course, you could be set to cross rivers and hills – just do not skip any steps; you need to develop solid confidence. Otherwise it could be a nightmare if your astral body succeeded in leaving your physical body and you were unable to bring it back for endless minutes.

Saturate your mind with only positive thoughts

If you can keep your mind blank, it is well and good. However, you and I know it is a tough call. So why not summon beautiful thoughts to lay foundation for a great astral experience? You do not want to be holding your breath on your astral travel after just watching a ghastly sight in a horror movie. Instead, you will do yourself a lot of good if you embark on your astral projection after reveling in good news or after reliving a successful experience of whatever nature.

Make your body boring and your astral body beautiful

This is the trick when you want to coax your astral body out. You need to visualize your body in a color that is pretty dull, and then have yourself focus on your astral body, in its very attractive and bright color, pulling itself out of that boring place that is your body.

Use a bright halo to keep off distractions

You need to be sure all your energies are protected and are being utilized only for your intended purpose – astral projection. So to keep off any forces that can sap your energies in a clandestine manner, it is important that you surround yourself with a white or yellow ring of light.

Know you are safe in the astral plane

Whatever your encounter, do not panic – nothing within the realm of astral plane is capable of hurting your mind or even your earthly body. For that matter, always keep calm and do not let any disruptive thoughts make you digress from your astral projection.

Imagine your physical body if you have to

In case the time comes when you want your astral body to have a reunion with your physical body and it seems a little stubborn, just visualize your physical body flying back from the astral plane as if in a flash; and there you will have your astral body back where it belongs. Remember time and distance are very different on the different planes. An hour on the physical world could be covered by a minute on the astral plane – or something like that.

Chapter 15: Integrating Your Experience

Once you return, you'll need to integrate your experience into your conscious awareness. You might come back with new understandings about yourself or the world. You might also see something that forces you to rethink your worldview and your beliefs. Be sure to take the time to thoroughly process your experiences before you move on and take in more.

Recording Your Experiences

It is best to keep a special journal for your astral travels. You might also want to use this journal to record your dreams as well. As soon as you awaken from your journey, record your experiences in your journal right away. If your body has immediate needs, make notes for yourself before you get up so that you don't forget anything. Revisit your old entries often so you can explore recurring themes and track your progress.

Understanding the Messages You Received and Interpreting What You Experienced

The most difficult part of the astral experience is understanding what we saw and felt. We often receive messages from our guides, from other beings, and from our own unconscious minds when we travel energetically.

A dream dictionary can help a lot when it comes to interpreting symbols you might have encountered. The meanings of these symbols can help you find the messages intended for you. For example, seeing an Egyptian ankh can mean that you need to pay more attention to the way that your own energy flows through your physical body.

You might have a very difficult time interpreting an especially cryptic message from someone. Write down the message and put it away for later. The meaning may become clear at a later time.

Working Through an Uncomfortable or Traumatic Experience

If you encountered an uncomfortable or even traumatic experience during your journey, you will need to take the time to work through it before you return to the astral realm. These experiences can stay with us if we fail to shake them, opening us up to similar experiences in the future.

Remember that you have the ability to protect yourself in any situation. Spend time being present in the physical world as you recover from your experience. If the encounter has to do with your own unconscious mind, seek out a trained professional, such as a therapist or life coach, who can help you work through and integrate the experience. Know that you are in control at all times and that you are perfectly safe.

Was It Real?

Many people need to have their experiences validated, especially at first. A common question when returning from an astral projection experience is, “Was my experience real?”

The answer to this question depends very much on how one defines reality. You can answer your own question by refining what reality means to you. However, the single most important thing to consider when it comes to answering this question is, how real was the effect that the experience had on you? Did it bring you real healing and real food for thought? If the impact on you and your psyche was real, then it matters very little whether the experience was objectively “real,” don’t you think?

Sharing Your Experiences

Everyone wants to tell someone about their experiences when they first return. This inclination is not so different from wanting to tell people about everything you did and saw while on vacation somewhere in the physical world. There’s nothing wrong with sharing your experiences with people who are open-minded and supportive of your practices.

Should you find your experience being rejected by someone you wish to tell, don't take it personally. Accepting an alternate reality in the spiritual world can completely upend someone's worldview, and making these sorts of changes is never easy. If someone reacts adversely to your story, their reaction is more about them than it is about you. Especially at first, try only to open up to people you know will receive your story positively, even if they only believe that you believe what happened was real.

Keep in mind that not all spiritual experiences are meant to be shared. If something especially sacred happens, or if a guide or spiritual being expressly tells you not to share a message or experience, remember to respect that boundary. Some wisdom is far too advanced for people who are uninitiated, and knowing it early will only harm them on their own journeys.

All in all, your return experience should be a positive one. With self-compassion, patience, and understanding, you can learn and grow so much from astral travel. Your newfound wisdom will enhance your everyday life and bring peace and satisfaction to your days. Be open to this experience, and good things are sure to follow.

Chapter 16: Techniques For Astral Projection

Once all your preparations are complete, you can finally move on to techniques with which to project your astral form.

The first few steps in entering a state conducive to projecting your astral form are pretty much the same:

Lie down in a comfortable position. If possible, take the same position that you've been using to practice the meditative breathing techniques. If you're using the moment before wakefulness, you may require more practice on catching yourself and extending that moment so that you can actively pursue AP when you're lulling yourself back to the hypnapompic state.

Cut down on any distractions around you. If possible, sleep in a different room or on the couch if you have a partner or spouse.

Keep noises, lights and movement around you to a minimum in order to better focus. When you lie down, first take a few moments to focus. Try to 'look through your eyelids;' visualize your surroundings without opening your eyes, through your closed eyes.

Start the meditative and visualization exercises that you've been practicing. The point is to keep going with these exercises until you feel more and more relaxed. Keep visualizing moving your astral body parts outside your physical body as you progress along these exercises. If you have trouble doing that, or focusing altogether, then try turning your attention to the spot just above and between your eyes – the position of the 'third eye,' or the 'mind's eye.' The objective here is to relax yourself while cutting out all distracting thoughts, keeping all focus onto one single thread of thought, either on a single fixed position or on a methodical visualization exercise. If that doesn't work for you either, you can also try focusing on the ringing sound in your ears in order to achieve the same result without outward distractions. The other major goal is to approach this experience in a positive manner, because your fears and worries may not only hold you back during projection, but may color your experience in the OBE as well.

Techniques During Hypnagogia

The objective during hypnagogia is to enter a state where it feels like your body is falling asleep, yet the exercises and focus on projecting are keeping your mind aware, but not completely awake – as I mentioned before, "mind awake, body asleep." In such a state, your mind will still be active but all sounds and lights around your physical body will have dulled and become muffled, if not completely disappeared. Instead, you'll be able to visualize the images in your head far more clearly, and may even see other images flashing across your 'mind's eye.' If you're able to reach this position and retain it without tipping over into sleep, then you're already making great progress. Continue the visualization exercises in which you move your astral body parts in and out of your physical body, turn by turn, as you 'stretch each part.'

Another technique that might help is to mentally visualize your own body as seen from above. It would help to imagine your own body as dull grey in color, with bright astral parts peeking out from time to time – a foot here, a hand there, a part of the forehead visible now, etc. Now continue the aforementioned visualization exercise, mentally lifting an astral body part out of your body and flexing and stretching it as you watch it happening from above. After you've gone through one complete cycle, visualize your astral body turning a complete 180 degrees inside your physical form: your astral head between your physical feet and your astral feet on both sides of your physical head. Continue another round of the same visualization exercises as before, this time imagining it to be far easier and lighter to do the same mental exercises.

Things to Remember at This Point

If you're already prepared and in a conducive state for astral projection, then you may start feeling a few things that might freak a new practitioner out, causing you to pull back. Even knowing them beforehand might not stop you from pulling back, but at least you'll know that you're at the cusp of a successful AP.

If you've done everything right to this point, and haven't fallen asleep, then you might start feeling a vibration in your body. It might go up and down, intensify and relax; it's a strange experience for someone who has never before experienced it. Just relax and let the vibrations wash over you. It's a sign that you're almost ready to start separating your astral body from your physical form.

If you haven't pulled back by now, try to control the vibrations and turn them up and down like the volume knob on a radio. Once the vibrations start, intensify your visualizations of moving your astral body out of your physical form. See if you can really start moving your astral body already.

If you're on your way to separation, you may also start hearing rushing sounds, or crackling and popping noises, or maybe even screams and other such sounds. Ignore them all. While they may be a bit disconcerting at first, they could no more hurt you than being shot with a child's water gun. Even if it is strange, you'll soon learn to tune it all out like other astral projectors. You may even sense the presence of other people or things around you; the same principle applies – no matter what may be present, it can't hurt you.

Instead, just concentrate on moving your astral limbs one by one, letting the vibrations continue their course.

Techniques for Separation

If you've made it through all the steps to this point, you should already be sensing movement in your astral body. For some people, separation comes easily, while others need a little more effort. There are quite a few ways by which you can detach yourself from your astral body:

If you're already sensing movement in your limbs, but can't fully detach yourself, you can use the roll-out method. Relax yourself – stop struggling – then simply turn and roll, as if you're falling out of bed. You should find yourself out of your body soon enough.

The rope method requires a bit of visualization, but is believed to work just as well. When your astral form has some freedom, picture a rope hanging down from your ceiling and dangling just above your chest. Grab onto the rope with both arms and pull yourself upward.

You can also use any solid objects around you to pull yourself out of your physical body. It doesn't quite matter if the object is within your reach. It acts more as a psychological crutch than a solid physical support anyway.

If you can free most of your body, but not the head, you can try bucking your body up and down like a bull trying to throw off a rider. The force will help you pop out of your body and free any astral parts that may have been stuck.

Another helpful technique is to simply will yourself to rise out of your body. The astral world responds strongly to will and thought, and is often full of junk material related to the same. You can find remnants of the will and thoughts of others as well, which were called into creation and will fade away if not sustained by thought in the physical world.

Things to Remember at This Point

At this point of projection, you need to move away from your physical body. The reason behind this is that your physical body still houses your ethereal body, which is believed to be electromagnetic in nature and can distort your astral sensations. You might feel a pull back toward your body, or feel like you're drunk or can't see anything clearly while still in the range of your ethereal body. After your separation, it's not necessary for you to be able to see your physical body, since it exists on a separate plane, or frequency, than your astral body – like colors made by different frequencies of light, or different frequencies of sound. Some practitioners even see their body in a different position than when they exited it – this is your ethereal body, rather than the physical one.

You should be able to sense things far more clearly once you're out of the electromagnetic range of your body. Now that you've initiated an OBE, you don't have to jump to anything right away, but can first spend some time learning more about your astral body. You can move through physical objects now, and limitations such as gravity no longer apply

– you can fly through your ceiling if you wish.

If you see or sense anyone or anything around you, don't be frightened. You can't be harmed and, if it's too disconcerting, you can leave at any point, or even will yourself back to your body. Regardless, nothing can harm or possess your physical body.

If you wish to travel farther, or have a specific destination or person in mind that you'd like to see while in the OBE, try willing yourself to that spot, or next to that person, or keep their image in mind and focus on it. That should be sufficient to get you there. Remember that astral projection is just as real as the sensations you experience while in the physical world – somewhat more so, in fact. It seems more like enhanced reality than a dream, trance or anything else of the sort. The more adept you become at AP, the more clearly you can observe everything around you.

If you spend too long in your OBE, your astral body will eventually be pulled back into your physical body on its own. If you wish to return before that, simply willing it to return to your body should be enough to break yourself out of the OBE.

How to Enter an OBE from a Dream

We'll discuss the full procedure here so you can develop this as a way to AP, if you so desire.

As discussed before, dreams are supposed to be windows created by the sub-conscious into the higher realms. In dreams, our own fear, desires, etc. form walls around us to give the dream structure and prevent us from sensing anything else outside. If you wish to enter an OBE through a dream, you should be able to sense and bring to your own attention that you're in a dream, which starts you off into your OBE.

To prepare yourself for this method, you should saturate your thoughts with the desire to project and reinforce yourself mentally whenever you can.

Also, whenever possible, ask yourself if you're in a dream. If you do this often enough, you may be able to consciously trigger the same question while in your dream.

While you're awake, jump a few times to show yourself that you're awake. If you're able to wrestle any control in a dream by asking yourself whether you're awake or dreaming, jumping will launch you off, rather than simply return you to the ground as happens when you're awake.

While this may sound a bit strange, you're basically trying to regain control by waking up your consciousness while in the dream. It's like being in a movie – not the viewing of a movie, but inside the actual movie – and then trying to develop free will, despite the script.

Once you've managed to wrestle control and launch your OBE, you should find yourself in your astral body, outside your physical form again. If you do manage to gain control but don't find yourself in your astral body, visualize yourself at the foot of your own bed, outside your body; that should make it happen.

Chapter 17: The Inhabitants Of The Astral Planes

When you are travelling on the astral planes you are going to meet a variety of beings. Some of these will have previously been humans, some will be teachers from higher planes and some will be actual beings that live on these planes and nowhere else.

Some of these beings will be positive and very nice whilst others can be negative and not as nice. Different beings have different personalities and different levels of intelligence. Almost all will have an agenda, that is a plan they are working towards, and most don't like being interfered with or bothered by visitors.

There are higher level beings such as angels, spirit masters and demi-gods. Some of these are friendly and helpful, some less so; some are neutral, some mischievous, some malicious and some are just plain nasty.

Life forms come in a wide variety of shapes and sizes on the astral plane ranging from beings that seem to be very animalistic and predatory in nature, kind of like the animals we find on the physical plane. These are often referred to as 'astral wildlife' because they are less intelligent and almost operate on instinct. Some of these are less than helpful towards visitors to the astral plane whereas others seem to actually enjoy tormenting visitors to their realm.

Given that by their very nature the astral planes are fluid you will find virtually anything there. Think of it like the sea – full of creatures, some of which are beautiful, some ugly, some friendly and some just waiting to bite your leg off! You will find plenty of other travellers out there too – some intentional and others who are projecting by accident.

Whilst you are travelling through the different planes you will occasionally find beings who are interested in interacting with you. Each plane has a kind of local inhabitant which live in very specific areas. Oftentimes they will not know of any dimensions or realities other than their own. They are usually amazed when they meet a traveller on the astral realms – think of an intrepid explorer making first contact with an Amazonian tribe. Some of the beings you meet will be well aware of the other dimensions and not have a lot of patience with travellers unless they approach with the right attitude. It could take you weeks or months to get some of these beings to stop ignoring you and start paying you attention. Treat everyone and everything you meet on the astral plane with respect.

Approaching astral beings that you are not known to is somewhat like approaching a complete stranger in the street. Most strangers will completely ignore people they don't know even when they are politely asked for the time or directions. Think of a busy New York street – how many people there would stop for a stranger asking questions? Many astral beings are not interested in getting involved with the affairs of travellers they don't know as they have much more important things to do.

You can sometimes meet up with other people who are consciously travelling, though a lot of the people you meet will be people who are not aware of the fact they are projecting on to the astral plane. Some of these do not realize they are on the astral plane and so don't realize they aren't bound by the same laws that tied them to physical reality.

Conclusion

Now that you have read all about astral projection and learned how it works, you should be ready to try it out for yourself. If you have any trepidation going into the process, understand that astral projection is completely safe. That is one of the best things about astral projection.

It is completely safe and you are always in control, so there is no reason to worry about anything bad happening to you. If you ever feel like you just need to be done with your out of body experience, then you simply will yourself back into your physical body and things are back to normal.

Having an entire different plane of existence to explore is an incredible thing. Many will not try this because they have a spirit of doubt, but realize that it could be the experience you have been waiting for.

If you have always felt that there is something more, beyond your physical self, then realize that you are right and the astral plane is waiting for you. Our physical world is a great thing and is a blessing in and of itself. We are not beings that are merely physical though.

We have a higher consciousness that is capable of transcending physical boundaries. By learning to use astral projection you are giving yourself an outlet to explore new areas that you have been longing to traverse for a long time, but never quite knew they existed.

Use the knowledge present in this report to inform you when looking to start your journey. It can a task learning how to control all of the aspects that go into astral projection. It doesn't have to feel overwhelming though.

This report showcases how beginners can take easy steps to becoming able to astral project. If you follow the steps closely and do so with an open mind and willing spirit you will have an out of body experience and you will be very happy by the new avenues you learn are out there to explore.

Exploration is really at the heart of astral projection. Those of us with a spirit that enjoys searching for new truths and exploring ground we haven't tread get excited about the prospects of astral projections. There are entire worlds out there that you can explore.

You can see things that you would have never thought of in your wildest dreams and moments of imagination. Being able to go through these places will open up your perspective and expand your mind in such a way that it will enrich your life permanently. No longer will you be able to see things from a shallow, jaded perspective.

Looking upon the universe with new eyes, the eyes of your astral body, will allow you to grow as a person. You will have spiritual and intellectual growth due to this process and the sum of its worth will be priceless.

So do not deny yourself this experience. Give the techniques a shot and see what it is you will discover. The three techniques provided will be able to help any beginner experience an astral projection for themselves.

If for some reason you do not want to try out the meditative techniques for achieving astral projections, there is always the lucid dreaming method. If you are already a lucid dreamer, then coming to understand the concepts behind astral projection and the astral plane can enrich your lucid dreaming experiences.

No matter your decision, the astral plane is out there and it is ready to be explored. Search your sense of curiosity and you'll find that you want to check it out. Embracing this new part of your life will be an interesting way to make life more intriguing.

Just knowing that you have somewhere to escape to when things get too stressed or dull in the physical world is very nice.

Learn to enjoy your time with astral projections and make the most out of exploring all of the possibilities. You'll be happy that you did.

Printed in the USA
CPSIA information can be obtained
at www.ICGtesting.com
LVHW010325200824
788752LV00021B/329